I love to write stories that will cross .... , than the recognition of my face ever will. Over time, I have changed, as most do. I have experienced loss and gain, I have been hurt and I have hurt. Life isn't exactly black and white, there is a whole lot of grey area and still so much color and beauty. To me, I am not this extremely fantastic person, but I am someone important. I have dreams and goals that someday maybe, just maybe, I will be okay. I don't dream of a world that is far off from what most people already have. Yet, I dream of a world where things are okay. I want to make a difference and show people that I am whomever I set my mind out to be.

I may struggle and may fail sometimes but in the end, I get right back up. I refuse to be someone's cookie-cutter mold of a teenager. Even if I wanted to be "perfect," there is no such thing. We all have a definition of what we think perfect looks like, yet no two people are the same and neither are their likes and dislikes. I am in college and I was pushed into a life of forced guidelines by my adopted family and the pressures of what they wanted. I was given no freedom of my mind. Sure, why not send a lesbian who already hates who she is to a small Catholic college in the middle of Vermont just because it's free for her. Yeah, not so sure that was a good idea. There wasn't much I knew about this school, that's for sure. Little did I know, this school just might make things worse. There was a program for "people like me." Damaged kids who struggled with the idea of what home was. Just great, right?

My life path seemed to be picked for me, the moment I said, "yes" to being adopted. From the moment I entered state's care, I lost all sense of my own identity and no choices would be mine again. No, this isn't me saying I was "lost in the system" or even that my safety was a mistake. It was me saying, that sometimes people are placed somewhere with people who understood them at one point. It's just sometimes you grow and you just have different dreams and goals that maybe, just maybe they are insane. Just at that point, you've already been through so much, nothing seems insane tp you anymore.

So my life didn't go as planned and I didn't end with the family I picked, I am thankful for them anyway because they gave me a better healthier foundation for life that I would create for myself one day.

So here is the story of a somewhat crazy, mediocre foster success. This story may be crazy, but it's mine.

When I was 13, the only thing I wanted was to be was myself and have that be good enough. At thirteen, I wanted things that most kids never thought of. I wanted a home. I put my father in jail because he hurt me. I thought the pain would stop there, I was dead wrong. He hurt me in ways I told myself I wouldn't ever speak out loud again. It's not even the sexual abuse that hurts anymore. It is the thought that I am now 17 telling a story, my story, over and over again. There are things that hurt me now, that did not hurt me back then. I am in college and I am learning serious relationships the right way now. May it be with a partner or even friends. It hurts because when I find the one, the one will get to love me romantically, they can never love all of me. There will be parts of me that I feel will never heal and most of them being parts of my heart. Parts of my heart that not even my adopted family seem to fill. It's like there's a hole that is stopping me from living and I can't seem to come up for air and just breathe because I am terrified. I am starting to understand that the broken parts of me will never be allowed to be loved fully.

"There won't ever be a family who loves me because I am broken." --This plays over and over in my head.-- There won't be a girl who wants a broken girlfriend because there are a lot of girls who are already whole out there. A girl will never want to touch me because parts of my body will cringe when they are touched and I will collapse the moment she starts to get close. Cringing because I am always afraid of being hurt, because how can people even want to touch me, knowing what happened. Sometimes when I shower I just stand there under the water. I let the water hit my skin because I don't want to even touch me. He ruined me.

Confession:

I am in college and I have never slept over at any of my friends' houses because I was afraid everyone else's' dad was like mine.

I had no idea what a real dad figure was, because mine, was awful. In the front of my mind, I knew that most people had "normal" parents and not parents that would hurt them.

I couldn't remove what the back of my mind kept telling myself.

Even at night, sleeping in my dorm room, I am terrified, I am terrified of every man I see even if I know they are good. Even the good, are capable of evil.

I am almost 18 and I am toxic, yet I hide it well. My friends all want to party and I just want to study. I want to sit alone and study because to me nothing bad can happen if that's all I am doing.

Someone asked why I wear my class ring on my ring finger and I gave them a reason. A reason some might find sad and others might think I am just intellectual. I am married to my education because it is the one thing that can't hurt me. If my education ends, it's because I left it or it was a job finished. It will forever be the only thing I can control. It was my savior when I was younger, won't it be forever? There will never be something that could fill the void that my families have caused. I am empty. I don't take this ring off ever and if I ever do, it'll be a miracle. The day the ring leaves me the finger, it means that I don't feel empty. To me that day will say, I will be okay. It won't mean that I don't value education just that I feel safe in the rest of the world now too.

I turn 18 in less than 40 minutes. Tomorrow I will be an adult. Yet, here I am sitting in my own little world and I have classes all day tomorrow anyway. It will really be the start of my "adult life." Classes from 8 to 8, what better way to spend a day, a full day that is all work and no play.

Last week I broke my foot, it was a really "shitty situation." My foot met a pile of dog poo, and as simple as the pain I felt, it was broken. One simple fall, just like my life, and my reputation ruined. Here a week later and people who look at me still laugh, like the pain isn't enough. If it isn't one thing in my life, it is another. I feel like I can't catch a break. Someone asked to sign my cast and I snapped at them. I said it was childish and that I can never grow up if my life is full of 'numbskulls.' How was I supposed to know what childish really was when I never had a real childhood, to begin with?

When I was 8, I remember asking for Law and Order to be put on so I could argue alongside the bad people. Or when I was 10, I remember knowing the words to Annie because I felt bad that no one seemed to love the little orphan. It's funny how things work out, isn't it?

What is the difference between being crazy and just having enough of your normal life? In a family of 6, I had 3 siblings. I had a younger brother, a younger sister, and an older sister. My family was one of those families where you are always together; it could be at a random party or even just sitting in the family room at grandmas watching television. There was something about my family that didn't seem like my friends' families. Everyone could be in the same room as one another but so disconnected, no one cared about what each person was doing or what was even going on in their lives. So close, yet so far away.

My older sister was not someone I could look up to for anything but she was my best friend. I had no one to look up to at home. With her being in my life, I had to be a child second, a grown-up first. Something about my sister was off and my entire family knew it. She was crazy and by crazy I mean she could be listed in like four of the diagnostics in the DSM (Diagnostic and Statistical Manual of Mental Disorders.) She was constantly making me take care of my little siblings because she knew our parents wouldn't. She knew they needed love and support and with everything going on, she knew it had to be me. The rest of our family was blindsided. Without even realizing it, I was trying to take care of her too. She knew she was the older sister and was supposed to be taking care of us, but she was sick and all of her trips to the retreat before this point weren't helping.

There are days when I feel like it's my fault she's broken. I am so awful to her that sometimes I hate myself for it. She's gay and I never let her live it down. My whole childhood living at home I used to make fun of her for loving girls and told her no one else would love her. I would look at her girlfriends when they would come over and I would just laugh because to me that's not what God wanted. God wanted his children to be pure and for them to love the opposite gender to give more children in this world a life. What I didn't know at the time was that I too was gay and that gay people can have families too. If anything they wanted so bad that they gave children who needed homes a place. I didn't know that my sister's problems weren't my fault. She was sick and there was nothing I could do about it. Her being gay wasn't wrong with her and that her mind was sick but not because of that. She had a lot going on but I was too young and had issues of my own I was going through. I didn't see what was happening to her because there was too much happening to me.

One morning when I was 12, I found her in her room, in a way that changed my life forever. When you're in 6th grade, it was not something you would understand. It was not something anyone would have any idea what to do when they saw it anyways my age didn't really matter.

My sister had overdosed on several different pills and she was just laying in her bed. She had overdosed before, but this time, it was different. It was bad, and I did not understand what was going on. It wasn't until I started jumping on her that she was foaming out of her mouth. When the foam had started coming out of the mouth her skin suddenly felt like pasta. It was cold and felt so wet, it was fragile and felt like it couldn't be broken. I thought she was being typical Nicole, just not wanting to go to school. I figured she was just being a jerk. So I jumped on her over and over again, until I realized, she wasn't faking it this time and the foam coming out of her mouth wasn't a joke. There was something wrong and I was scared. I was scared I was going to lose her because she was my sister and I needed her. I ran out to my parents, screaming. They rushed me off to school so I didn't have to see what was going on. But that right there was just normal to me. I saw her foaming out of her mouth and I thought that she was dying right under my feet. At that moment, I couldn't even think of the last thing I said to her. All I could think of was I am 12 years old and the last thing I would have said to her was probably hurtful. I was scared and at that moment, I honestly didn't know that this wasn't the only time I had ever been this scared.

The sad thing is this was probably the best parenting choice they ever made. The choice to rush the rest of us kids out of the house, so we wouldn't have to see what was going to happen to Nicole.

I remember it like it was yesterday, even though it wasn't the first time that this happened, it was the first time I saw it. It was the time that I realized something, if she wanted to die and was not able to, neither could I. I wanted to stop being hurt and death seemed like the only way out of it. But all the pain and things going on inside of her, if that wasn't enough to die, then I really wouldn't be able to.

My mom had told me that if it wasn't for me jumping on her, my older sister's heart would have stopped and she would have died. The actual thought of the word death had scared me. My older sister was not exactly the type of person I could look up to because she was sick. I still loved her; she was my older sister.

The days she went crazy, were the days I would run to school because that was my safe place from everything going on at home. It was my safe place from her, from my parents, from having to protect my little siblings.It was pretty much the only time I was my age. My safe place was in my classroom surrounded by my real friends and my teachers. Those were the people whom I grew attached to and in the summer, it was always hard.

 I was constantly trying to escape from everything.I would go away, but the temporary style wasn't cutting it. I couldn't keep going back to bruises and pain. What happened if one day if all the abuse or I went too far and just killed myself who knows what the outcome would be. I was small, he was big, it's not rocket science, anything could happen. That's when I knew if I couldn't speak up something bad would happen. I needed to protect myself, more importantly, my little brother and sister. At the same time, my older sister meant the world to me and she needed help too, just in a different way. That is why I spoke up. I spoke up at that moment because I was done. I wanted to die but I couldn't. I couldn't kill myself because if I left no one would do anything and there would be no one stopping the little ones from getting hurt. I just couldn't take it myself anymore.There was nothing else I could do, no one knows how much more I could take. I was broken and that was everything I could do, who knows if the pain would ever stop for me, but I couldn't let it even begin for them. They had their whole lives ahead of them, they needed to be protected and I couldn't do it anymore. I couldn't protect them because it was turning into a point where I couldn't even protect myself.

 There were times I would make a mess in my room in case something happened and nothing was left of me. Sometimes I would pack a bag with my stuff and put some of my siblings' stuff in it too. I would run away with them and everything would be okay. Other times, I figured maybe I just wasn't loved and if I left it would all suddenly be over. They would be fine and I would okay.

Everything I had ever known was the hurt and the craziness of life. I knew that people were sick and there was never anything that anyone could do. It was the end of all I had ever known and I wanted it. I wanted it to end right there. I wanted to be okay. I wasn't sure what that was but I knew that it must be me feeling a lot better than I did. I needed safety and I loved my family but when you're not safe, sometimes love isn't enough. They say if you love something let it go. I loved my family more than anything but the love I was getting back, wasn't healthy or safe.

2009- Late August

It was a really beautiful day outside. The weather was gorgeous and yet it seemed to be so cloudy. I am not sure if these clouds were a figment of how scared I was as usual or if it wasn't really that nice of a day that. Either way, it didn't matter, my whole life was about to change and I had no idea what was going to even happen. I went to school that morning and was just getting used to my schedule and my teachers.

We were sitting in the gym getting acquainted and someone came in and said I was wanted in the office, I thought was in trouble and I stood up and my heart sank. I looked back at my gym teacher and she smiled I left. I sat down in the office and the police and the counselor, some lady I didn't know and the principle were all there.

They started asking questions and one moment after another the pit of my stomach began to fill. I had been sitting in the guidance office all day at this point, talking, being looked at with eyes full of sadness by people I didn't know.

I was sitting in a room that seemed to smell of desperation and sweat from all of the kids who were in trouble or needed to "talk their problems over." Was I going to get in trouble for letting my dad hurt me all of those years? Was something bad going to happen? I had no idea what is going to happen, I just want my sister. I want my sister so I can make sure she is okay. Will I see my younger siblings? Where was Nicole since she didn't always go to school, was she okay? I just want my dog, he makes everything feel better. The end of the day came and I wasn't allowed to return to classes that day because they wanted to make sure I was okay, they wanted me to know what was happening and just thought me sitting in there was a good idea. Little did they know, I should have been in class because I felt safer there, less numb.

The end of the day the officer looked at me and told me he was going to bring his truck to the front of the building and he was going to walk me out and bring me somewhere safe. Walking out I saw so many people from my class that just looked at me. Someone yelled at me asking why I didn't return to class, someone else was asking if that was my dad and I didn't understand why. I climbed into his truck and there was a bar separating the front from the back. Was I in trouble? I know they said I wasn't but I started to feel sick and I was scared anyway. I suddenly couldn't breathe.

Maybe if I kept my mouth shut, it would have stopped on its own? Maybe I would be okay in the long run. Maybe just maybe I can pretend I never said anything and I could just say that I was confused and didn't know what I was talking about. I could pretend that I had some issue where I was crazy and I didn't know what my other body said. I am scared because I don't know what is going to happen. Where am I going to end up now? Coal. My dog. I could only think in my head. What is going to happen to my boy? Will my dog be okay? What is going to happen to him? Can I bring him with me? I want my dog, maybe he will make everything better.

It was that moment, I knew I was alone and my whole life was shattering under my feet. Sometimes I sat there wondering if the abuse would be okay just so things could stay mine. My brother and sisters would be mine, I would have my dog and I would at least get to predict what would happen to me. It was like clockwork anyway. The abuse would come and go. I could escape that pain by running away sometimes, it wasn't a permanent fix, but over time maybe it all would work itself out. I would just wait until I was old enough to leave and I would bring the little kids with me or maybe Nicole would take us when she got a little older. It would all be okay, wouldn't it? It would only be a few more years until she could leave.

My body feels so numb right now as I am sitting in the van of a lady who smells like lettuce and sweat. The lady that was in the office told me that I was going to be staying with her for a while.

EL and TJ would be too, so we won't be split up. She said Nicole wasn't going anywhere, that Nicole and my mom were furious with me for making up this big story. Was my mom crazy? She was there when it happened, how could she think I was crazy. She watched me with dad. She took pictures sometimes with her camera. She watched just like I did when I saw every time dad hit her. I would try to look away but he made me watch if he knew I was right there. He would hit me when he saw me close my eyes. That was when it was easy because I could always lie and say the bruises and the scars were from Nicole, everyone knew she was crazy. I could just blame her for everything going on. Maybe if she was normal, things would be okay.

Picking up my little siblings was weird. When I went to the classroom they said EL was in the gym. So I went to get her from the gym, but when I got to the gym, they told me I needed identification to pick her up. But they knew me, she was my gym teacher last year. She knew who I was and that EL was my sister. Why couldn't I get her? She was my sister, I picked her up last week even. The lady ended up coming to the gym and then we all just walked out. It was stupid, I could have just got her, it wasn't like I knew where to go anyways.

When we got to her house, it was weird. It was clean and she said we would be sitting at the table for dinner soon. I didn't really ever sit at a table and eat together unless it was a holiday. Although even then, we never all sat together but tonight, we would all be sitting together.

For the meantime, I had my little brother and sister and I could watch them make sure they were okay. They didn't quite know what was going on but I am not sure I quite understood it either.

What was going on? Were they going to keep us with this family forever? What would happen to my older sister, my dog, my parents? The only thing I was for sure of at that moment was that I hated this woman and her husband.

I didn't believe in God or whoever they kept preaching about. I didn't understand why he was allowed to be a foster parent and be a minister at the same time. Wasn't that like crossing some line of church and state or something?

All I knew was if they didn't get me out of this house I would go insane. Stupid me thought if they moved me, they would move my brother and sister too. They were moved first and then these crazy people had it in their head I was staying with them for a long time so they took me paint shopping so I could paint "my room." Little did they know I was also leaving and I hoped to never see these people again. Just like that, I was moved and I am not sure this was much better.

October 2009; A few months later

Tomorrow is my birthday and I haven't really heard from my family. Did they know I was okay? I didn't live with those religious people anymore so it is not like I was going to throw a religion in their face.

My aunt sent me a card, she was the only one who cared about me. I folded it up and I kept it in my pocket because it had money in it. That money was my way out. All I needed was a bank because I would cash it and run away.

I didn't feel safe. This new lady the state placed me with was insane. She was older and not even that friendly. Before me, she lived alone I wouldn't be shocked if she had lived alone since her daughter was a teenager because this woman was bitter and just seemed sad. My younger siblings were moved, so now I was alone and I had no idea where they were, they were moved somewhere else.

I thought the first couple that I was placed with was bad, looking back, I don't think religious people seem so bad anymore. I feel like I am in jail here.

My routine kinda sucks. I wake up and get ready for school. I then eat some fruit (which is disgusting by the way) and then wait for the bus. Middle school is weird, but it's not so bad. While I wait for the bus the lady sits on her porch, I think she knows I want to run away. I wouldn't do it before school though, that's dumb. After school, I take a different bus to my babysitter.

Let's be real, who has a babysitter at almost 13 years old?

Then she would pick me up from the sitters, I would go home into my room and sit there until dinner. Then at dinner, I would come out of my room and eat the same 5 meals pretty much over and over again and I would eat by myself because she ate on her own time by herself. After dinner, I would go back to my room and take a shower. After my shower, I sit in my room and then go to sleep. This lady isn't very social, I don't think she likes me but it's okay because I am not too fond of her either. Maybe she will knit herself a cocoon and eventually morph into something more pleasant.

It's my birthday. I am 13 today. I guess it's not bad being a teenager, I feel I got my teen attitude early. They say teens are the worst. I woke up early and I don't feel any different. I am all ready for school but my work is supposed to pick me up from school today and take me to the movies. I haven't really been to the movies much in my life. My parents used to say they were overpriced and movies would eventually end up on the TV that was already paid for. Most of the things all of my friends were seeing, I couldn't. My parents were strict about what I would watch on TV which is weird because they let me watch stuff that they should have been nervous. Stuff that would make me think something was wrong with my life.

Well, that was a blow. My worker got me from school and we went to the baseball field and she gave me a cupcake (which I wasn't in the mood for) and some presents. I know she asked if I liked them and I told her yes but who gives a 13-year-old a giant bag of sugary candy and a ton of soda for their birthday? She couldn't take me to the movies like we planned because something came up so we went back so I would hang out in her office for the afternoon. So I am just kinda doing homework in the same storage like the sitting room they put me the first day everything happened. This other lady who works here told me she would be in shortly to hang out.

Well, hanging out with this lady was playing Candy Land. Which she cheated, she won every game and it was my birthday; she should have let me win. She was nice though, if anything, she is the only nice person in this office sometimes. She didn't treat me like a little kid, I was a teenager to her. I mean obviously minus the game, but there weren't many options in this office.

When I got home, the lady I live with had a couple of gifts for me on my bed. They were clothes. There was a couple of sweatshirts which were all too small and a card. She gave me a belt too, it had hearts on it. She told me at dinner that it would help with my pants being a little big. They weren't my style but at dinner, I said thank you and that was it.

It was pretty much any other day. I eat, I go to my room, I shower, I sleep.

Wasn't this all supposed to be compassion and love? Wasn't the point of getting me away from my life was so I would feel safe and comfortable and cared for? If that's the case, I don't. No, this lady isn't hurting me but I feel alone. Like I don't exactly matter to anyone anymore.

Nobody knows me anyways

I have friends who I tell some things, I have people who work with me, who I tell some things. Some more than others. But then there are the people, I don't tell anything. They see me and I see them. But to them, I am just me or at least what they see. I feel like I don't belong in this world. That somewhere, something messed up and I was born by accident. Is it bad that I don't feel like I have a place? I mean I know you're a stupid book and don't have answers I just feel so useless and out of place. Maybe I was just a science experiment that escaped, or I was a real result of time warping. I mean that's a thing right? I mean of course it isn't but still, ya know?

I got this stupid workbook from my therapist, she said it would me get my feelings and stuff out there. Then every so often she would read this book and then we would have something to talk about. I don't like to tell her anything so I guess this could work. Don't get me wrong, she's a nice lady but let's be real. She doesn't want to know what happened, it always makes people act weird around me. If she knew what was going on in my mind or all the things that happened to me, she would be just like everyone else and say sorry and tell me over and over again it'll be okay. That things will "get better." I call bullcrap. Nothing is okay now and it won't be.

I just wish I didn't have to keep telling my story over and over again, it makes me feel sick. It's like the moment I start talking about it I want to puke. I feel fine for the most part just a little sick and gross until I look into someone's eyes when I am telling my story and they give me this look. It's a look as though they feel sorry for me. That my whole life was bad but it wasn't all bad. I got sisters and a brother. I had lots of pets and I had a dog once who I miss a lot. No it wasn't good but it's not their fault, right? It's not like she or anyone else hurt me. They didn't even know who I was until this all happened so why they even care is beyond me.

As I write in the book I think:

12: A peaceful place in my mind….A sunset on the beach in the spring. Listening to the waves roll up on shore, or just sitting in the middle of nowhere away from everyone, by myself.
13: I have ignored my feelings forever and sometimes I wish I had not ignored them. But I feel like I would be judged. I had felt that I was alone and no one would listen to me. Then there

are days where I think if I didn't do something, I would explode into a trillion little pieces and then I would be everywhere and then people would know. It's not like Humpty Dumpty, I didn't sit a wall I wasn't made to break but I am so fragile, that I could anyway.

14: Reading helps, it makes my mind far less dangerous. Have you ever tried living in the mind of a 14-year-old girl? I don't think so. I guess I could try to read for an hour or two every single day. Then if I can't handle these stupid emotions I would write how I feel down in a special notebook and then I would call my gym teacher or my advocate or even my counselor. I guess.

I skipped exercise 15 because it was dumb and I was not going to answer the question.

16: I don't have any sexual concerns, I started reading books in the library that kind of help me. Oh, and I have been reading stuff online. I found a pen pal that is helping me learn about myself because I am too scared to ask these questions myself. I guess you could say my concerns are bigger and more awkward but not sex. Sex is forever forbidden from me. I don't think I could ever let someone touch me or see me naked. They would see all the bruises and scars, they would know. They would know I am broken and there's nothing good to me.

Looks like I will be skipping 17 too, these questions are so invasive. (isn't that the point?)

18: I have a nightmare, every single night it is the same exact thing. It started about 2 months ago. I can't talk about it because then I just cry and how am I supposed to be strong if all I do is, cry. As for my concentration, I can't do it all the time. Sometimes when people talk to me, I just don't hear it. It's not that I choose not to I just can't simply take everything in lately. Typically if someone says certain things I just start having flashbacks and then I really can't focus.(PTSD)

Sometimes, I am just sitting around and the events play over and over in my head. It's like sometimes my mind is cluttered and the only thing that comes out is things that will break me down. I feel emotional all the time like it is never ending fear and craziness. Aren't 14-year-olds supposed to be out having the time of their lives? Meeting new people and enjoying each day and not constantly worrying about where I am going to end up. My counselor at school kept on asking if I had anger outbursts or panic attacks even some depression and all I can say is no. That I am fine. I feel guilty that someone else's mom has to take care of me and now they have to share because my parents didn't do their job. They hurt me and now someone else has to fix their damage. What if I can't be fixed?

I don't really control my feelings well. I won't lie. I keep them to myself that way I am not a burden and other people don't have to deal with them. It's my problem. When I do want to talk to people about how I feel, I don't know who is there who really cares to help me. When it comes to how I feel, I keep my wall up and I act like a jerk and I know that. No one will ever see this but I hope they know I am sorry. I am easily hurt and sometimes, I question it if I am worth it.

Is it weird that when I am sitting at home and nobody's around, I feel like someone is there? It's like I hear something and then automatically I think, oh my word, someone is here. I think I am crazy and sometimes I feel like if I just ran away, it would all be okay. No one would have to worry because I wouldn't be a burden. Then when someone really is there, I wouldn't know because I would be out being paranoid somewhere else.

We got asked a question in school today. If there was ever a time we wished we were someone else. Some kids said yes they want to be richer, some said they liked who they were and then there was a few of us, who sat silent. No thoughts erupted from our minds that we were willing to share. Me, I would love to be someone else. Someone less needy, who needs less attention and who can grow up without growing down. That is so good!I know that sounds weird but I feel like I am not really growing up because I never got the chance to be little.

Today, I feel worthless, yesterday too. I thought by getting away from the abuse that I would stop wanting to die. But now, I realize I don't want to die as much or for the same reasons. My family hates me. If I ever have kids what do I tell them? Oh, your real grandpa hurt me and his family loved him more than me. That even though he could hurt his own daughter, his family didn't care. What kind of life would my kids ever have? Would they have a family other than me?

Ugh, food. I have no desire to eat lately. If I get fat I am going to end up just like my family. If they don't love me, I have no desire to be anything like them. I want to be better. They think they are great people yet, I didn't pick what happened. If I could, I would have made my family normal. I wouldn't have been abused or had a sister who ran away or was trying to kill herself all the time.

The rest of the family would love everyone and not let any pain occur to any of us. We would eat and be happy. But no, the only time the family even cared was when food was around. So why eat? It didn't protect me before, what good is eating now? At this point, I have had an eating disorder for a while and I don't see it stopping any time soon. Some people are afraid of clowns or spiders, I am afraid of weight. Every time I look at a scale I cry and get sick even more. Then when I see the numbers going down it's like a high to me. I get excited and feel so good. But that isn't my only problem, I have plenty of those these days.

I had a lapse today. I cut my wrist and I decided I would just wear a hoodie so no one could see it. It's getting harder and harder to cover them up because it is getting warmer outside. Between the nightmares, the confusion, the trying to be somewhere else and the biggest problem, wanting to be someone else, I am struggling. What 14-year old says that?

I have been having the same nightmare for 68 days. Every single night, like clockwork for some reason, I have the same nightmare. Someone said talking about it would help but how can you talk about something you don't understand?

I feel depressed lately and I won't admit that to anyone. Sometimes, I don't have the intention to die but after I cut myself I just wish it hit something then all of the pain would be gone. I started cutting somewhere else on my body so that way people can't see it. I am too fat for shorts that are too short so I just wear them long enough to cover all of my hideous fat and now my cuts. It's different now. I used to have to hide the bruises from my dad or sister. If they weren't hide-able, I would have to make up a story as to how I got it because my father said people wouldn't understand if I told them the truth. I remember when my sister punched me in the arm I got a really nice bruise and I told my teacher I fell out of a tree. How did I get in a tree to fall anyways or the question no one else seemed to be asking was where were my parents for all of these crazy moments? That's right, they were there, because I wasn't falling out of trees or playing a little too hard.

I wake up some mornings and feel numb. Today, I reach into my desk and on my way out of my room I take the drawer out. I reach into the desk space where the drawer was and pull out a blade, I put the drawer back and go into the bathroom. I turn on the shower almost all the way to red as I undress. I get in the shower and sit down. As the water is hitting my body making my skin a bright shade of red, I start carving at my skin. As the heat from the burning water numbs my skin, the blade dragging across my skin seems to make no difference. I don't feel the pain anymore. It's not until I look down and I can no longer see my skin but the trails of blood turning my entire shower floor red. Just because I can't feel it I go in once more and I let out a cry. Someone knocks on the door asking if I'm okay and I just tell out, "yeah sorry I just got myself shaving."

A little while later, I decided it would be best to throw away all of my sharp things and get rid of the temptation. I need to stop. I am done crying and feeling alone. No one feels sorry for me because I did this. I told what he did, protecting myself and my family. But why I am acting like this, cutting, not eating, throwing up when I do, I am not helping anyone especially myself. Why do I blame myself for everything? It's not like I asked my father to hurt me.

While I am learning to be good to myself I am starting to "date" random people. Let's be real, dating at this age isn't really dating is it? I won't lie. I do it to fit in with people my age. Even though I have no desire to be with these people.

For a while, I had a secret relationship and fake boyfriends. I told the boys that I wasn't really with them but people would think we were because I was with someone else and no one else could know. Plus, they were okay with it when I told them I was dating a girl. I wasn't quite sure why, but over time I learned guys liked the idea of that kind of thing. I guess it sounds trashy but I wasn't sure what I was doing or why.

I feel uncomfortable when the sex talk comes up. Even more than normal lately. Sex since I found out what it was and how wrong my dad was for it, it's been disgusting. But the idea of having sex makes my skin crawl now, how can I ever make love when he took it from me. The ability to be pure for love. I mentioned to my counselor that I had a girlfriend and no one knew because I had a fake boyfriend. She wasn't shocked but she didn't judge me. She was one of the first people I came out to anyway. When I told her about a year beforehand she wasn't shocked and didn't judge me which was nice. I thought she would judge me like everyone else. It's weird, people my age are having boyfriends and doing things with them. Some of them are worried about "being good." I don't know what that means exactly but I am not too worried. It doesn't help that I am not into guys so I can't force myself all over one just to feel like my peers. I just want to be normal and have someone love me. I mean honestly, would anyone ever love me anyway?

There was a time, I used to lie to my parents for my sister. I know I wasn't a good liar but my parents didn't care too much to be angry about it. They honestly didn't seem to care much at all when it came to her. My mom made the comment once that she was a free spirit and she'd be home when she had the munchies or something. When I was younger, I had no idea what that even was but I went with it.

My older sister ran away one time and I told my parents she went to her friends' house down the street. I said she went to study and we all knew that was a lie, she went to get high. I told my parents the lie because if they knew I knew why she left, I would get smacked for knowing, and I would also get in twice the trouble because I didn't run to them and tattle right away.

I don't know why they cared when I knew and didn't say anything but if I didn't know and neither did they, they wouldn't ask questions when she came back either way. Then there was a time where my sister told me she wanted to kill my dad and I tattled on her because she wanted him dead, but I loved him, I was his little girl. But he had EL, so I don't get it really. It's funny because now I wish she had killed him. He ruined me, he ruined my future. Why didn't I want him dead? He wasn't a good person, all he did was hurt me and everyone in my life. He was a hero in my town and everyone loved him though. He was a firefighter in two different departments, he was studying to become an EMT, he bounced from job to job. I loved him, but why? Why did I want to die so much but let him live?

Dear Dad,

*14 almost 15 years of being hurt, the pain of not knowing fully
or even understanding the real reason why.*
*Why can't/ won't you just say sorry? I don't understand why it
was me? Was it just me even?*
*You may have officially lost me when DCF took me but the
day I was testifying in court it stood out to me. You didn't even
care to be there. I wanted to puke that day. You were hurting
me and you didn't even care.*
I have nothing to say anymore.

-Courtney

Looking back at things now, I don't know how I or
someone else didn't notice something was going on. My family
was really close. But at the same time, everyone was so far
away in their minds. It was like everyone cared but only about
themselves.

Feelings in my family never mattered and I don't know
why that never seemed odd to me. My family was extremely
physical, I just thought it was normal. What was normal to me,
was horrifying to others because the difference is, I had no
idea how many laws were being broken. I wasn't even sure I

knew what the difference between illegal and legal was. Looking back at life, I see an entire family who was broken. No one knew better because they were all quitters. God forbid I don't even know the most educated person because they all picked having kids over graduating anything. The simple truth was, that no one cared about the bigger things because self-absorption was the end result of teen pregnancy.Don't get me wrong, some people can have kids at any age and still do so much, but not them, I guess.

I could think of a million things that could be said or done in the past and I am still young. I am scared for life because I live in a constant state of fear of ending up like they all did. They weren't all terrible, but the ones who were, it took me pain to realize it.

Every single time someone tells me I am going to be a good parent one day, I panic quite a bit because there is no way I could have a child because I would just ruin their life. I may not be the worst parent but what if I put my child through pure hell like my family did to me.

I didn't realize it when I was younger but as I got older I realized it and the more I learned, the more I hated my life. As I got older the only thing I could tell was that my life was completely different from what my friends' lives were like.

I have a family who makes money to love me, my real family abused me and the rest left, and I am now scared no one will ever be able to love me, for me.

Dear father,

I am 19 now and you may always be part of the reason I was born. But you're not my dad. You see, a dad is someone who cares for their children. Anyone can create a kid, but it takes a real dad to protect and cherish his little ones. He will you teach you those skills you need to grow and be loved. He is involved in the transition from being someone who was selfish, to one who is now selfless. He is the person who teaches you to accept the fact that it's really no longer about you anymore, that life is large.

You did not teach me those things but in fact, your absence did. You are sitting in jail being punished for what you did. But I refuse to let myself be punished for anything about you any longer. You taught me unhealthy relationships and showed me pain. Up until now, I thought you ruined me. But instead, I was allowing it.

I met someone great who shows me, love. Love that is real and full of emotion. That great thing can happen even when it doesn't seem possible. This is me telling you, I am over everything. I refuse to let you define me. The things I learned growing up and was scared to change had to go. I am capable of so much more than that.

When I have kids of my own, which I plan on doing with the one I love, I will know how to be a mother, more importantly, a mom. I've seen what bad parents are my entire life and at my age and what I have seen now that I am older, I have seen good parents as well. Maybe not in one person, but yet collected skills from different parents I have seen in my life. I won't say you ruined me anymore. Of course, you took my life, my innocence, my childhood, but you won't take anything from me any longer. You gave me life, you gave me tools to know what bad can be. Just because it was unhealthy doesn't mean that I didn't learn from it when I was old enough to process it.

I am not asking for a sorry anymore because I know you're not. In my own way, I am kind of telling you that if you wanted to hurt me, you lost. So here's the end, you won but also, here is the end, you lost. You may have thought you were invincible, but you are not. When you hurt someone, you get hurt too. You had your fun when I was younger and then you lost. I lost, I got my life taken from me. I won because now that I am my own version of me, I am okay and that is no thanks to you. It's over.

Court.

Stronger Apart

I didn't speak much of my adopted family, not because I didn't care, but because they weren't exactly awful. We just had different views.

They allowed me to grow, experience and learn. I won't say much about them in this story because that's a different part of me. I walked away from that family because they made me weak in different ways.

They were part of me and they did become part of me, but even though they were part of my life, they weren't exactly a good fit for me at that time. I spent years trying to defend my adopted sisters for whatever the case may be.

I decided to start working my butt off to become the person that would fit in their family but that would never happen. I didn't fit in. I wasn't one of them even though I shared a name now, I lived there for years and yet I was nothing like any of them.

My dreams, my goals, no part of me fit in. I spent so long in that family trying to do and be something I wasn't and had no desire of wanting. For those years, I wasn't growing in ways I should. I was sick. I was sick in the way, I had an eating disorder, I was a cutter, I was always depressed. I hated myself for being gay, I was miserable and everyone around me knew, except for them.

In those years, I dated girls from Tumblr or my school. I tried being someone different just because I couldn't quite be myself. Even though everyone said they approved, they didn't. My love life wasn't a discussion and when it was I was told I was confused or hadn't found the right guy. Going out to see my girlfriend when I would have one in town wasn't as easy as it was for my sisters.

Learning things or asking questions in my house wasn't easy for me because I felt trapped. I never told anyone this except for my closest friends but I always questioned, if foster care and the adoption didn't bring in money, would they have still picked me to care for? Would anyone?

As I grow, I thank them. I thank them for letting me grow and thrive in their home, I thank them for being a family and for being stepping stones in my path. I love them dearly, but I wasn't lucky the first time with my family and not even the second with them.

I didn't get my happy ending right then but I will one day and that's why, I don't gloat on those moments, my story took a step past this all and continued.

Dear mother,

I am 19 and happily living my life. I recently allowed you back in my life and I have no regrets towards it. Knowing you understand it isn't easy for me and nothing about this is natural to me anymore, it means a lot that you just 'let it happen.' I originally was only allowing you back in my life for EL but I realized it was more than that.

As much as I try to admit it, I look so much like you. I want to know where I come from. I want to know my background and my real story of who I was.

Now that I am old enough to know and understand, I want to dive in head first, but I know that isn't healthy.

I started dating someone who you've recently met. I brought her back for a reason. I wanted to include you in my life and the choices I am making. Regardless of my spot in the family, I never want anyone to feel like they are left out. That my life is full of people and no two people mean the same thing in any way shape or form. Some are just there, some teach lessons, some are to be taught, some come and some stay. Everyone in life is different.

You met someone I was involved with. I brought you into my life not because I wanted to be hurt again but because I want to show you that I know it's all not your fault, what love can be, what family can be and that even though I was adopted and finished being raised by other people, you gave me life.

I was born because of you, and no, I am not your biggest fan but I want you to know, I don't hate you. I won't be telling you everything that goes on in my life or saying we will be close but I am saying I won't block you out. It's taken me a long time to get to where I am at but it's better than not knowing me at all I think.
-Courtney

When I went away to college my eating disorder grew at first because I was trying so hard to get used to my schedule, dining hall hours, make friends, do all my service hours, it was a lot.

I quickly realized why I fought so hard to end my eating disorder this last year that I fought hard again to kick my bad habit. I was healthy, with a good weight and happy, I couldn't go down that road again.

I started finding things that I liked again and made my mind so busy that I didn't have time to think about it all. Since I wasn't a fan of eating in the dining hall and it was barely open anyways I started making more and more lunch and dinner in my room. As I was eating and always on my feet, I realized I didn't need to make myself sick or starve myself, I was happy the way I was and I refused to ever let myself go back down that road again.

After college, I moved out on my own in a city I grew to love for a while. But I wasn't ready. I wasn't ready to be on my own. I made friends, lost friends. I grew but I also was stuck. My relationship was bumpy and even though I was in love, my world was stuck and I was declining.

I wasn't dealing with my own emotional health. I stopped caring about myself because I was indeed trying to keep a relationship that I wanted so bad but even more so I was just trying to make everyone around me happy. She to me was my person. The person who I finally learned what family was, what happiness could be. I made such a big decision on living in a new place alone, but I didn't stop to think if I was ready for all of that. So even though I loved my new city, I had my relationship I was fighting for and all of my friends, I was losing myself.

Then when things went sour, I ran away. I ran to my birth mom because, at the time, I told myself that if someone was going to hurt me, why not let it be her? Why not let it be the one who at least gave me life. I was afraid of screwing up so much that I figured nothing could go wrong. I kept telling myself there was no pressure. My siblings were too young to care what I was doing, my mom wasn't some successful doctor or anything. I felt like I had a chance to be someone when I didn't feel so much pressure anymore.

It's getting warmer but my life seems to be getting colder when I decided to leave college with just my associates to pursue other dreams. I finally felt like I had a place in the world and a direction to go. I went from Vermont to New York to become something. Little did I know, having a vision didn't mean it would always happen. One thing after another I was moving again. From one city to another and then another, until it blew, it blew up in my face.

Sitting there, I was fighting with my family and my little brother threatened me because I was finally yelling at my mother. No, it might not have just been about that moment. Maybe I was finally reacting to my whole life but that's not the point. My brother didn't like the idea of me yelling at my mom, but little did he know what we were even fighting about. He stepped in and told me he was going to fight me and if I didn't shut up he would kill me. *Now I know what you're thinking*, no I don't think he really would hurt me, but it's the idea.

At the moment he said that it brought me back all those years. He looks so much like my father. At that moment, I was scared and I ran again because the depression, the anxiety, the PTSD it all came rushing back. I didn't know where else to go so I called my older sister and ran to her.

The biggest moment for me is after all these years, she was finally protecting me. My older sister was finally being the person I needed all these years. She was becoming not only my friend but the older figure I needed. Not because she was a lawyer or a doctor or anything but because this whole time, I just needed my sister and I just wanted to feel like I was doing something or being something that someone was proud of.

I was constantly feeling like I was disappointing everyone in my life. I knew I needed her. She got through her depression and even though I didn't want to admit it, I was bad again and wasn't sure at that point if I would get through mine.

With my relationship being a mess and my friends all being far away, I felt alone and scared. I was stuck in my head and losing control of my mind and my heart. I was bad and I knew I just needed to lay low and just have some mental space but also see what it was like to be on the other side. The last time I spent time with my sister was that night she came back from her coma after overdosing I was 12 then, I was 20 now. If she could do it, I wanted to see how and feel that I could too.

It had been nearly 2 years at this point since my eating disorder was fully gone. I didn't tell many people I was having issues, I didn't even tell my therapist I was struggling sometimes because I felt like I was constantly disappointing everyone. People were working so hard in my life for me yet I wasn't even able to hold it together for myself.

There was a day when I was at my sisters' and my mother came to visit and she looked at me and at the time I didn't realize why my heart sank until a little while later. The look she gave me at that moment was the last look she gave me in the courtroom the day of trial when my father was being sentenced to prison. It was the look she gave me when she said she was sorry and she loved me. I felt a lot of emotions at that moment and some of them, were peace because I was learning not to hate her, but to just be at peace with what happened and just try and look forward.

At this point, my life is a mess, the girl I thought I would marry one day, decided that us not being together was a good idea anymore. My life felt shattered. I spent so long fighting for this relationship because I was happy. I was in love and then it was gone.

At this point, I was miserable. Nothing in my life seemed to be going right, it was a mess. The life I was trying so hard to create, was shattering underneath my feet and I didn't know what else to do anymore. I was afraid because everything seemed to be going wrong that I would turn down a spiral again and so I ran.

This time I wasn't running away because it was fun, I was running to become something. Moving from the north to the south would be a big change for a lot of reasons. I needed it though, I needed to take a step back and finally get help in a different way though.

My whole life so far was a series of events decided by someone else or irrationally deciding something based on everything else. It's been hard to be an adult or grown up when truly, I was never taught how. I never had a real childhood so I missed out on a lot. Yet, I grew up so fast, I didn't learn how to do much for myself, others, or the world. This move wasn't supposed to be all fun but a wakeup call and finally getting loved by people in my life who genuinely just want to see me thrive in life and be the most successful person I can.

Dear father,

I am 21 now and my life is very different now. Someone asked how I felt about you last year and I didn't know how to answer it or what I felt entirely. Now, I can say, I don't know what I truly feel.

You gave me life and taught me what not to do so for that I am thankful. I am thankful that there are a thousand miles between us and you can longer hurt me. At one point the abuse even though it has stopped and been years I could still feel the pain in some of my body. That pain is no longer a feeling but a memory I will always have. It's weird to think I feel more punished than I feel you are. You are sitting in a jail doing who knows what all day. Getting free health care, free meals, not being an actual part of society. Your biggest issues are within those walls. Mine? My issues are what's happening in the real world. I can't hide behind walls just because when I was little you ruined my life. I don't get to just be a space taken up. I have to be something and I am terrified of everything. I am 21 and I still jump when men look at me even if I know they are good people or their sexual identity has no desire to be a with a woman.

I went to a male gay club recently for a birthday and when a stranger grabbed my arm it brought me back to those days. I wanted to scream but I knew it wasn't like that. I spend a lot of time secretly crying because I don't have the answers for everything. Some days I want to hate you and others I find myself trying to find a reason that you did all of the things you did. I've settled for not knowing and not exactly hating you either. I simply just choose to say I don't have a dad anymore and that everything happened only happened to me because the world knew I could handle it.

-Signed, Courtney

After years of not being given an answer or knowing why everything happened, I sometimes look at stories of people who have been through similar things to see if they know.

I watched a documentary once and the abuser stated he did all of the things he did because he had someone in his mind telling him to. I've read other stories where the abuser has once abused himself and couldn't control his urges.

When I first went to college I wanted to study behavioral psychology to learn more about the brain and human urge control but I realized I spent half of my life so far sitting in therapy processing what I've been through and how to cope. I adore the lady who helped me through everything but I don't think trying to find answers or go about that way solves everything for everyone.

Sure I can spend all this time learning about the brain and why people act the way they do and things but do we really know? I admire every therapist, counselor or whatever out there but that wasn't for me. I don't think the answers are so simple that they can relate or describe every situation.

I used to love therapy because I'd learn I'd be okay and that it wasn't my fault. I liked the feeling of being safe and knowing I had someone who believed in me, understood why I was broken and so torn. I liked understanding all of the things she would tell me like that I wasn't alone or that one day the pain would go away and I would feel "normal." She understood that there is no such thing as normal but over time you become your own version of normal and just cope. That's all things really are after all of the abuse and neglect. You're forced to learn to cope every single day.

Some days you will look in a mirror and you might hate and blame yourself even though it's been years and it wasn't your fault. Other days you won't even think about it because you are so much more than the abuse and everything you endured. That's just it though, life for those who have struggled through a situation have a harder time than someone that didn't, but the end of the day, we all have our own story. Some people will come with this broken baggage and just try to be loved anyway. Others will have baggage but it won't be the same. Life's a game, not everyone will play by the rules, some won't finish the game, some hop from game to game. That's why life is so hard because it's a crazy big world we live in and some view rules and safety as things to be broken.

I sometimes struggle with the idea of who I am now. I look at everything that's happened. That my birth parents didn't work out, my adopted parents didn't work out, that must mean it's me. But I am reminded that it didn't work with my birth parents because they weren't good. My adopted parents are lovely people who I am very thankful to have had in my life, but they aren't for me.

I am so set in the idea of wanting to be my own person, have my own story and succeed that I am not willing to risk who I want to be because it wasn't the idea someone else had for me.

I look bad now and wonder if I ever even heard my parents say they were proud of me. My adopted parents did a few times, but they were things they wanted me to do. Sure I wanted to graduate and go to college but no matter how hard I worked I never felt like I was truly good enough.

When I was little I was in art shows all the time, I won a poster contest for the governor for fire safety, I had amazing grades and tried my best in everything, I never got praise. When I got older I didn't do anything seem to matter. I got asked to compete in a beauty pageant and ended up tagging along with a friend and her mom. Her mom helped me get ready. They tried to guide me and show me as much support as they could. But my friend was also competing so how can you cheer for two girls in the same competition coming against each other? When I got home that night it was so late and no one was awake to hear how it went or how much I totally loved it. My friends' mom could have me look like a clown and gave me the ugliest dress so I would lose but I didn't care, I really loved doing it. I remember on the day of my first rugby game, I was so excited to be playing. To be doing something so different, yet none of my adopted family came to watch. Everyone else had someone cheering, I didn't. Part of would look into the crowd just hoping to see someone there cheering for me, but there never was. I was just another player on a team of a ton of other girls. After the match, I remember calling home because there was something wrong with my car and they came right away and then went right back home. I got home and they were just eating take out. That day, I honestly just went to my room at the end of the day and cried. I didn't feel like I had support in anything I wanted to pursue. I didn't think anything I tried to find the passion to do would ever be good enough.

It took years to come to terms with everything in life, one moment I would feel so low and felt like I had no support. The next, I felt like it didn't matter who was standing by me because I stood by myself. I look back at the sports I quit, the opportunities I didn't take, the people I distanced myself from and I realize it's all history. I don't believe in one God or another, but it's my life and it was given to me because I could handle it. The friends who left, the girls who broke my heart, the boys whose hearts I broke, it's life. Every little thing adds up. Someone else gained a best friend, others fell in love and the rest realized that life won't always give them what they want. It's hard one day waking up and suddenly life is not exactly what you had in mind.

When I was 14, I told myself I was never living anywhere but Vermont. When I was 16, I was getting ready to embark on a trip of a lifetime. At 18, I was in college and finally putting myself first. At 21, I moved across the country to start over. No, starting over isn't always the answer but it does answer some questions. Does moving away make the pain stop? No. Part of me will always know what happened, who came, who left. I won't be able to meet the people I already know again. Is moving away giving up? No. Moving away isn't giving up. If anything, its giving in. Giving in to the idea you are worth great things. So what, it didn't work for someone else or people don't agree with your choice. What matters is you understand why you left. Did I run away? No. I ran from one thing to another but I wasn't running away. I was running to something. I was running to myself. I needed space and fresh air. No, not the crisp mountain air you get on a lovely spring morning. But air to grow. My heart will forever be in the mountains looking off into the distance but the air I now breathe will be cleaner for my mind.

Sometimes, small-town kids aren't made for the mountains and dead-end roads. Sometimes the dead silence and the sounds of only crickets or animals drives your mind crazy. Sometimes, just sometimes, they want bustling streets and somewhere that the silence doesn't drive insane, they want a city with life and opportunity that you can't get from just sitting around hoping one will fall into your lap. I tell myself that I will regret the chances I don't take.

Once you think about it, you can't take the small town out of the girl. There are moments I sit outside and just look up at the sky. I look at the moon and tell myself, the moon is the same everywhere you are so just because you leave, doesn't mean you have to change. Not everyone appreciates the beauty of the moon but those who do love it for all it is, for what it looks like even though it always looks different. I take a step back and realize, it's okay. It's okay that not everyone sees the beauty in everything, it just leaves more room for me to admire it.

I tell myself that I am worth something even though I grew up being told I wasn't. That the abuse doesn't define me and I am worth it. The abuse was out of my control but my life is not. I am the author of my own story, we all are. So we don't like the beginning, we can't change what's written in stone. We can change what hasn't happened and make it what we want. Who cares what people think the greatest ventures come from the unknown. Let it be known, that you are living your best life and don't let anyone create a future for you that you don't want. Speak up when you want to be heard and be quiet because it may be your story, but you are not always the star. Find happiness in life and find life in happiness, you get one shot.

The biggest thing I have learned is that some people can't write their story because they are afraid to live. I'm thankful everyday for everyone in my life who didn't let me cut too deep or let me be too sad. I am thankful I was never fully alone because I wasn't strong enough to handle the weight on my shoulders. I have seen those I love lose their battle and it makes me wish they had the support I did and didn't think that was the only way to go, but sometimes they feel that is the only choice they have. Sometimes, the fight is only half the battle and there is just too much weight and it can't all be taken away. I have felt the loss of those around me and the pain feels like another bag of rocks being added to my load. It gives me so much emotion knowing how those who lose the fight feel but at the same time it gives me so much more hope to stay knowing how much the loss feels for those in my life. I am thankful to be alive knowing I do have loved ones who didn't get to stay somewhere out there looking for out for me.

Today, I look back at the years in my life that now seem like so much more. I think of all of the teachers I encountered who took care of me when I was younger and didn't even know it. I look at the way some of them would smile at me and little did they know that smile was the only one I would see. So these are letters to them, to my heroes. Not all heroes wear capes or uniforms. The school was my safe haven and to most, it was just a place for learning. The school was like home for me.

My elementary school was full of souls who made me. My third-grade teacher pushed me in ways I would one day be thankful for but in that, at the moment I hated her for. I wasn't one to want exercise. Morning gym was my savior, it gave me a reason to be at school earlier each morning. Fourth grade gave me bike club that would teach me that finding an outlet would be so much more than just art. My teachers laugh and personality showed me that laughing is the best medicine and that one day, I will be okay.

My fifth/ sixth-grade teachers were my soul. Since it was divided class, the one teacher taught me to fight. If you have a passion stick it out. Ride your bike to the store, make projects that would scare other teachers because they aren't typical. To be whoever you want. The other, she was my savior. I told her these many years following my 6th grade moving up ceremony. That I don't know where I would be without her. I needed a home but not the type with four walls. I needed someone to be proud of me and make the idea of growing up okay. She was more than just a teacher but family to me. She showed me writing was my home and when I did it I could be safe. She went above and beyond her job and made me feel safe for years. If I could give her one thing, it would be for her so proud of me and I owe my life to her. She may not know, but she saved me. For years following, she was my soul. Meaning I felt safe when she was around and I could be myself and be okay when she was around. She will always my savior and so will my paraeducator from that year. They watched me grow and held my hand when I was scared and helped me grow when I was afraid to even breathe.

Then middle school, I hated gym class but my gym teacher was more than just that. I no longer had the teachers from the elementary school who I knew. Who made me feel safe and important. But ever since the first day I was taken into custody, she was what I now associated with me being safe. No, she wasn't the one who took me out of my parents but she was there and made sure every single day I was okay. If I was afraid of class, she would walk me there. If I was in class and felt like exploding, she would let me just go sit in her office. When the case finally went to trial she went above and beyond her duty and went with me. She held my hand when I felt like I was alone.

Then came high school and the moment I walked into the doors, I wanted to walk right back out. I found home in my 9th-grade humanities class by my social studies teacher and upstairs in my seminar by that teacher. My 9th-grade social studies teacher was the first one to understand me in high school. She didn't fluff my life or baby me. She gave me a guide when I needed one but wasn't afraid to push me when I was stuck. For years I felt stuck but no one else wanted to push but she saw something in me and I thank her for pushing me. My seminar teacher was this goofy ball of energy that I adored. I didn't know why I clicked with her so well but I did. She protected me before I even knew I needed it. She gave me an outlet to escape to but pushed me in the right direction. She never let me be stuck. When I was sad, she knew how to fix it and when I was being stubborn, she knew how to stop it. She gave me my first autographed book by my favorite author, that would quickly become the possession I value most in life. She understood me before I understood myself. She held my hand through the ups and the downs and never left my side.

But I don't chalk all my success to my teachers but a great deal of it, you bet I do. When everything first happened I was assigned a support figure and to her (and my therapist, of course) I owe the most gratitude from back home. So these letters, are for them. Thank you. If one day you're reading this you know who you are.

For my advocate, thank you. You were a hand to hold when my family couldn't be there. You were a guide when I was young and source when I was older. You gave me my best friend even if that was crossing boundaries. You understood that kids will be kids and you can't change that. You were always there for me and made sure of it. You made sure I was never alone and never allowed me to be alone in my head either. I told you everything because you were my safety. I wasn't afraid when you were around because you were more than just my advocate, you were family. You knew me better than most and understood me more then maybe I even understand myself.I could always count on you when I wanted to feel like I mattered. You were proud of me when no one else seemed to be. You were there for ways I couldn't have imagined, and I would have been so lost if it wasn't for you and everything you had done for me. I found that family is more than we usually think and that sometimes the people we start off not wanting to like become the most important. You never gave up on me even when I was an awful rude teenager. So thank you for being, you.

To my therapist. There is so much I could say but I don't know how. You gave me a safe place and helped me process and deal with everything. You gave me a safe place to be my authentic self even though my life was a mess. You showed me it was okay. You made me feel welcome in the world and like I wasn't an outcast or weird or broken. When I came out, you helped me process and understand. You were more than just my therapist but my guide. Without you, I wouldn't be okay today. No, you don't have special powers that can fix what it is broken but you gave me the power to glue the pieces together and become whole again. I think back at all the times I would sit in your office and want nothing more then to just ball my eyes out and it's more powerful knowing you would have been there for me even if it wasn't your job. That speaks volumes knowing that you go above and beyond your job duties. You let me cope and deal at my own pace. You didn't rush me to be okay and to talk, you let me go at my pace and stood by me when things were really bad. You are a hero of your own kind. You saved me. So thank you, for everything.

The letter that means the most, is one I can't write just yet. But I will say this, to my aunt and uncle. Thank you. I can't say what for because baby steps are where I am at but just know, I wouldn't be here without you. Thank you for protecting me, for loving me, and for being the parents I didn't get. Thank you for being my people. All of my success and positive change is all thanks to you.

Sometimes, we forget that we are just one person. I wouldn't be me without all of the people I have had in my life. It's okay to not have all the answers and to not be okay all of the time. It's okay to take baby steps and to go at you own pace. Dealing with trauma isn't easy. No two stories are the same and no two people are alike. One might struggle with something that someone else doesn't. That's the thing about even the parts of life that shouldn't happen is we can try to understand and cope but it's not easy. We can seek help and we can seek answers but we can only learn so much. The rest is healing from within yourself. Finding things that work for you and help you. No one can dictate your pace or progress because only you know when you're okay.

There are moments I think back to everything since I was taken from my parents and I tell myself that everything in life won't be easy. That the hard part may not ever fully be over, but it's how you deal with it. Learning how to cope is only half the battle. Life is weird in the idea that what you have already been through can't be changed. The future is what matters now, it's never set in stone so if you're unhappy. Change it.

So my story doesn't end here. I am young, I have a lot of life left to live. I have been through so much already in my life that I wonder what the rest will be like. Sometimes, I even get bored with things in my life because it's finally not crazy. I have space to breathe, a future to look forward to, choices to make. I am living a life that is my own yet for the first time in my whole life, I finally feel like it is mine to live. I was honestly afraid. I had no idea that I would get a chance to feel what happiness was like, but I am. No, not every single day is full of sunshine for my mind but the ones that are, seem so bright and full of potential. Yes, sometimes it's not easy to wake up and I admit I am scared from time to time but I can't let that dictate my life.

Each day is and will be different. I will have ups and downs but at the end of the day, I choose to smile because I am alive. Every day I make the choice to stay and fight the battle and that is a good enough reason to smile. I may not be where I always thought I would be at my age but that's okay. Every single person is different and had their own timeline and so what if I don't have all of the things most people my age have, all that matters is that I am happy and every single day I wake up living my best authentic life. I have been through so much that for now, it's okay if I am taking a step back. Like they say, even hurricanes go through the most beautiful places. So my life was a hurricane and now it's time to rebuild what was broken and honestly, sometimes what's rebuilt is better than what was there in the first place.

Printed in Great Britain
by Amazon